CALM COLORING

new seasons®
a division of Publications International, Ltd.

Let's get social!

 @Publications_International

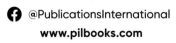 @PublicationsInternational

www.pilbooks.com

"The essence of love is kindness."
—Robert Louis Stevenson

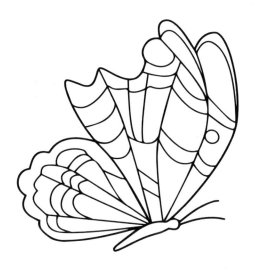

"Books are the quietest and most constant of friends; they are the most accessible and wisest of counselors, and the most patient of teachers."
—Charles W. Eliot

Enjoy all of creation, each leaf and flower
and every small pebble along the way.

Gratitude turns what we
have into enough.

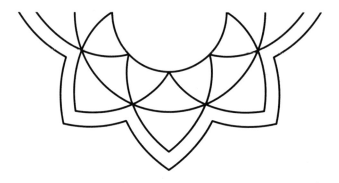

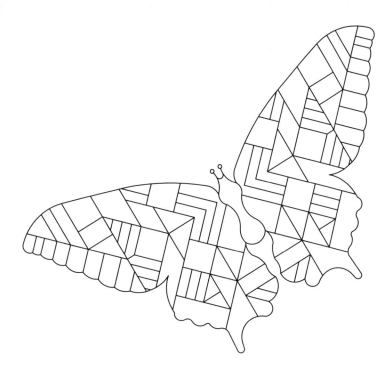

"It is eternity now. I am in the midst of it. It is about me in the sunshine;
I am in it, as the butterfly in the light-laden air. Nothing has to come,
it is now. Now is eternity; now is the immortal life."
—Richard Jeffries

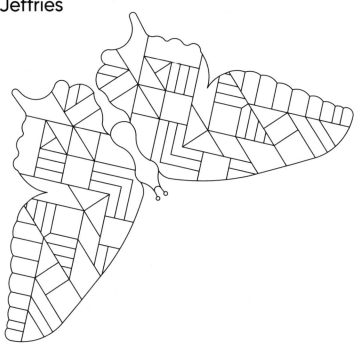

"With an eye made quiet by the power of harmony and the deep power of joy, we see into the lives of things."
—William Wordsworth

Seek comfort in the garden, seek adventure in the wilderness, but seek the truth within yourself.

"All glory comes from daring to begin."
—Anonymous

"The world acquired a new interest when birds appeared, for the presence of birds at any time is magical in effect. They are magicians that transform every scene; make every desert a garden of delights."
—Charles C. Abbott

"A sensitive plant in a garden grew,
And the young winds fed it with silvery dew."
—Percy Bysshe Shelley

"The cheerful birds their airy carols sing,
And the whole year is one eternal spring."
—Ovid

"A quiet mind cureth all."
—Robert Burton

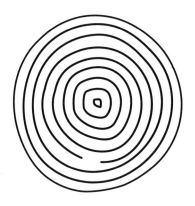

The best view comes after the hardest climb.

"I'm not afraid of storms, for I'm learning how to sail my ship."
—Louisa May Alcott

"Great works are performed not by strength but by perseverance."
—Samuel Johnson

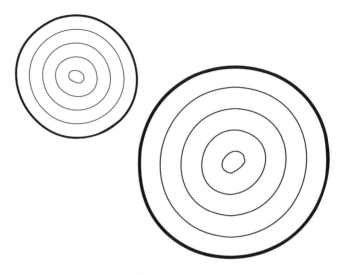

"It's not what you look at that
matters, it's what you see."
—Henry David Thoreau

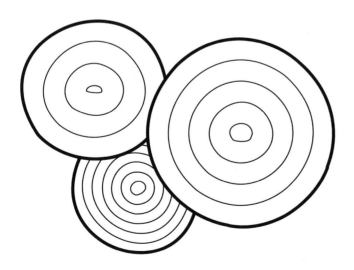

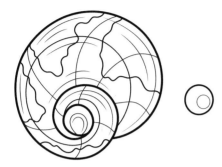

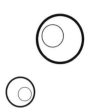

"Rivers and the inhabitants of the watery elements
are made for wise men to contemplate and for fools
to pass by without consideration."
—Izaak Walton

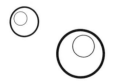

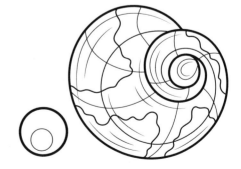

"To live happily is an inward power of the soul."
—Marcus Aurelius

"The birds with their plumage and their notes are in harmony with the flowers."
—Henry David Thoreau

"Nothing can bring you peace but yourself."
—Ralph Waldo Emerson

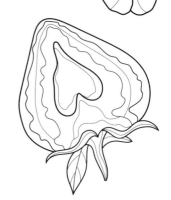

"Each flower is a soul opening out to nature."
—Gérard de Nerval

"Be glad of life because it gives you the chance to love,
and to work, and to play and to look up at the stars."
—Henry van Dyke

Without seeming rhyme or reason, hope allays the soul's worries with the certainty of hummingbirds, who know precisely the day to fly south.

"There are finer fish in the sea
than have ever been caught."
—Irish Proverb

"There is no duty we so much underrate
as the duty of being happy."
—Robert Louis Stevenson

"To look into the depths of the sea is to behold
the imagination of the Unknown."
—Victor Hugo

Don't postpone joy. Even in the midst
of the storm, the flower grows.

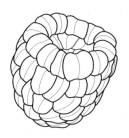

"Nothing is sweeter than love, nothing stronger,
nothing higher, nothing wider, nothing more pleasant,
nothing fuller or nothing better in heaven or earth."
—Thomas à Kempis

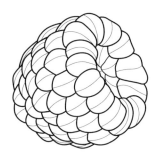

"The divine nature is perfection; and to be nearest to the divine nature is to be nearest to perfection."
—Xenophon

Train your mind to see the good in everything.

"Earth laughs in flowers."
—Ralph Waldo Emerson

"Faith is the force of life."
—Leo Tolstoy

Don't look back and agonize over roads not taken,
dreams not pursued. Look ahead to the future to
new roads to discover and new dreams to fulfill.

The song of the universe is sung through
each of us. Its notes, our dreams and visions;
its melody, how far we've come.

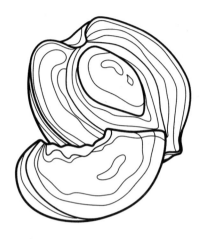

"Gratitude is a fruit of great cultivation."
—Samuel Johnson

"Instead of a gem or a flower, cast the gift of a
lovely thought into the heart of a friend."
—George MacDonald

"Forgiveness is the fragrance the violet sheds
on the heel that has crushed it."
—Mark Twain

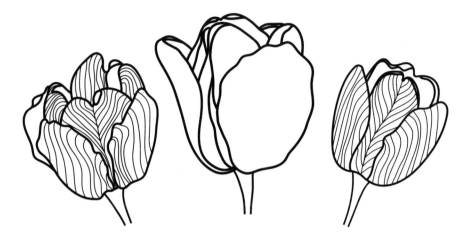

"The sun does not shine for a few trees and
flowers, but for the wide world's joy."
—Henry Ward Beecher

"Turn your face to the sun and the shadows fall behind you."
—Maori Proverb

"The fairest flowers have cheered me with their sweet breath, fresh dew and fragrant leaves have been ever ready for me, gentle hands to tend, kindly hearts to love."
—Louisa May Alcott

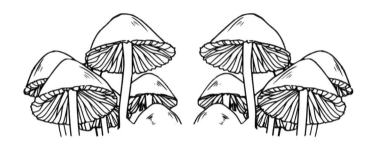

"Surely there is something in the unruffled calm of nature that overawes our little anxieties and doubts: the sight of the deep-blue sky, and the clustering stars above, seem to impart a quiet to the mind."
—Jonathan Edwards

Embrace the hope of each new morning, and the last ray of sunshine to fall at day's end.

"Peace comes from within. Do not seek it without."
—Buddha

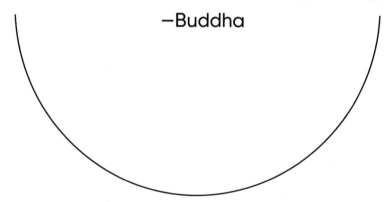

"Nature speaks in symbols and in signs."
—John Greenleaf Whittier

"It is not in the still calm of life, or the repose of a pacific station, that great characters are formed. Great necessities call out great virtues."
—Abigail Adams

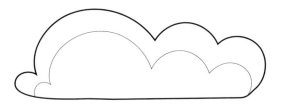

Attitude is the mind's paintbrush.
It can color any situation.

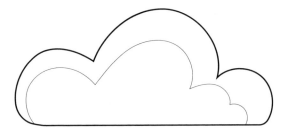

"Love is a flower that grows in any soil, works its sweet miracles undaunted by autumn frost or winter snow, blooming fair and fragrant all the year, and blessing those who give and those who receive."
—Louisa May Alcott

The beauty of creation inspires me to live a life
where I, too, can create something beautiful.

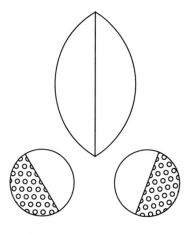

Listen with your ears, eyes,
and heart wide open.

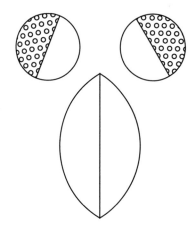

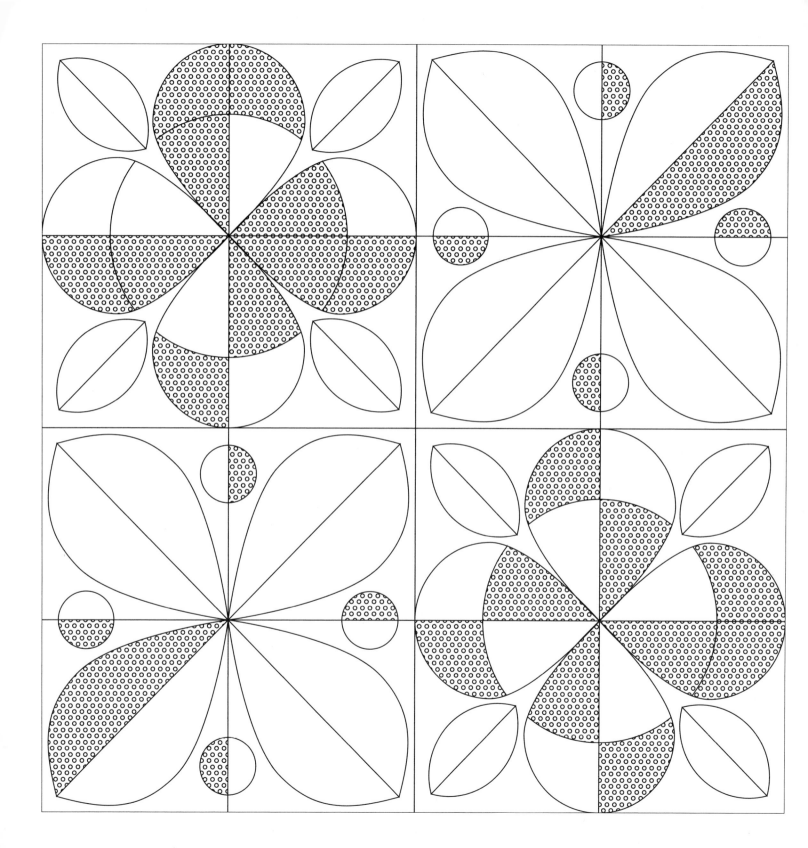

"Moments make the hues in which years are colored."
—Edward Bulwer-Lytton

"The world is but a canvas to our imaginations."
—Henry David Thoreau

In the solitude of a natural setting, the heart discovers serenity, the soul knows abiding peace, and the spirit finds renewal.

Learn from yesterday, live for
today, hope for tomorrow.

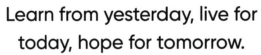

Quiet time restores our bodies, our souls, and
our health. If you can, set aside time each
day to let go of your worries and cares and
just rest in calmness and peace.

Every moment we are alive is full of reasons to sing out in joyful gratitude. Every breath we are given is a reminder that the glory of life is at hand. In the people we love, in the beauty of nature, in the golden sun that rises each morning—miracles are everywhere.

Keep taking steps that move you forward and
you'll always be heading in the right direction.

Take time to make your soul happy.

A small thing, as simple as a breath of fresh air, supports the changes we make: The present is breathing in, and the past is exhalation.

Hope blooms like a beautiful
rose amidst the thorns of life.

"Fill the cup of happiness for others, and there will
be enough overflowing to fill yours to the brim."
—Rose Pastor Stokes

"The greatest thing in this world is not so much where we are, but in what direction we are moving."
—Oliver Wendell Holmes

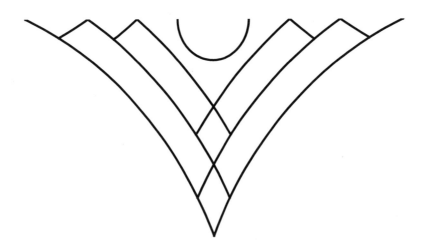

"Friendship is a sheltering tree."
—Samuel Taylor Coleridge

"Never be in a hurry; do everything quietly in a calm spirit. Do not lose your inner peace for anything whatsoever, even if your whole world seems upset."
—Francis de Sales